YOU CANNOT SAVE HERE

COVER DESIGN by Andrew Sargus Klein
COVER ART by Geography of Robots
TYPOGRAPHY by Barbara Shaw

ISBN 978-1-941551-49-3

Library of Congress Cataloging-in-Publication Data

Names: Moll, Tonee Mae
Title: You cannot save here : poems / Tonee Mae Moll.
Other titles: You cannot save here (Compilation)
Description: Second edition | Washington, D.C. : Washington Writers'
  Publishing House, [2025] | Summary: "Winner of the 2022 Jean Feldman
  Poetry Prize from the Washington Writers' Publishing House, You Cannot
  Save Here is a collection of poems about how we live when each day feels
  like the world is ending. The poems ask what we do with the small
  moments that matter when so much around us—climate disaster, gun
  violence, pandemics, wars—makes these days feel apocalyptic. The book
  is a bit speculative and a bit confessional. It's queer, punk, and woven
  tightly with cultural allusion, from visual art to video games, pop
  culture to counter culture"— Provided by publisher
Identifiers: LCCN 2025007462 (print) | LCCN 2025007463 (ebook) | ISBN
  9781941551493 paperback | ISBN 9781941551509 epub
Subjects: LCGFT: Poetry
Classification: LCC PS3613.O458 Y68 2025 (print) | LCC PS3613.O458
  (ebook) | DDC 811/.6—dc23/eng/20250325
LC record available at https://lccn.loc.gov/2025007462
LC ebook record available at https://lccn.loc.gov/2025007463

WASHINGTON WRITERS' PUBLISHING HOUSE
2814 5th Street, NE, #1301
Washington, D.C. 20017

You Cannot Save Here

POEMS

Tonee Mae Moll

Washington Writers' Publishing House
Washington, D.C.

TABLE OF CONTENTS

III.

I.

I used to wait for the explosion, the big crash, the sudden chaos that would destroy the neighborhood. Instead, things are unraveling, disintegrating bit by bit.

Parable of the Sower, Octavia Butler (1993)

YOU CANNOT SAVE HERE

—the first day of The End
I don't do anything just
sit in the dimness of midday
room with unopened blinds

lament the lack of energy
needed to fry up egg alternative
open the fridge more frequently
than is practical. Eventually a sunshower

taps on the porch, breaking through
soot-soaked sky, and the small dog
at my feet needs a walk, so we suit up
each in mismatched mackintosh

and along the way duck sauce
cuplettes bloom from tossed off
takeout bag while broken warblers
call out car-alarm songs

In the distance I mistake
discarded t-shirt caught
on almost-budded branch
for late spring's first heron

The End sounds so familiar, like
So Eden sank to grief,
So dawn goes down to day
like Sunday. like a half-gone song

IF YOU SEE ME, WEEP

"Wenn du mich siehst, dann weine"
—Hunger stones, 1616

On the Elbe, exposed stones
reappear to sing of hunger
days to come

Somewhere closer to home
the coast has become a funeral
torch, a miles-wide pyre

Crackling out of an old radio
a long-gone crooner cries:
Enjoy yourself—it's later than you think

and you realize the song's been on
for decades, so standing on a catastrophic
shore it's hard to tell if a wail

feels too much or not enough
Sunset arrives early, and you decide
against hand tattoos, S-T-A-Y C-A-L-M

in a shrinking city, in a failing country
your tiny comforts feel precarious
You keep horizon eyes as you eat

late summer peach with cheap
shiraz, roll a poem into empty
bottle knowing every song

a latent hunger
stone, an unease tucked
beneath tomorrow's seam

You suck your fingers
sticky with dread, begin to hum:
Enjoy yourself——

YOU CANNOT SAVE HERE

Someone is crying in a Denny's
blessed be, it isn't me this time

Picking at the stack of jam packets
someone is stomaching the end

of something, I'm sure. I am overflowing
with run-of-the-mill existentialism

My coffee cools, and I watch while
he tries to bridle a sob, an ugly

sucking bawl over his Moons
Over My Hammy. A gazelle

of a boy bounds over and almost
whispers *are you ready for the check, sir*

I wish I could summon the courage
to feel in places I am not permitted

I'm not trying to Bukowski you—I have
no revelation as my partner scrolls through

Twitter and I finger a waning mozz stick
while a B-side Bee Gee's track plays

I'm just gathering endings, great and small
sack cloth and ashes and all that

YOU CANNOT SAVE HERE

After Mary Oliver and John Berger

Whole blocks give way to blight
and I darn my favorite sweater
I'm lying, I pay someone
to darn my favorite sweater
I'm lying, I buy a new sweater
assuming endless supply

skip my long run day and stay
indoors, watch *ways of seeing*
while working out a body
I can't save in the long run
a body I can't afford to resolve
and won't before the walls rot

The top of the world packs up
and goes more quickly than we
predict. I'm grinding experience
points, the mirror sends me
on a side quest, and I clutch my gut
like a hamburger, murmur: *180 by April*

Hail Mary, full of grace, I keep trying
to do the *one wild and precious life* thing
make something lavender of the hooded
crow's wailing cries, fold together
a family of lovers who know the most
poetic ways of barricading the doors

We get on with it, as the fires start, focus
on breathing, anything sacred: the holiness
of hands, of handjobs, of starting gardens
of garlic climbing through the floorboards
more tender names for orgies, for Aprils
for the last time the earth bows to the Sun

YOU CANNOT SAVE HERE

                                              We go on
In the bread-colored land called *workplace*
I am trashcan fire in Conference Room A—
I am sure I know nothing about the borders
along which we split self from form

I am too often convinced
I am the only ache
in this throng of neutral suits—
no one asks my pronouns

but I'm learning to trust
no one who knows
for sure the name
for the space their body negates

All I know is I am
the sharp scent of clementine
peel lingering on thewy hands
I wish were smaller

I remind myself not to believe
in anything as predictable as the tide—
self should be approximate
like when and where
a fish will devour a hook

THE OFFICE OF TOMORROW

Hip-
high
broomsedge
savannahs
reclaiming the oak
veneer of our desks, the fallen
walls, plasterboard partitions beaten into powder
rare earth electronics returned
replaced with rough stone;
all progress
rendered
wind
thrown

NEW PRAYER FOR LOVE IN THE ANTHROPOCENE

i.

BLESSED are the thirst trap poets
built bodies extending before
wall mirror, post-gym,
eyes-fixed on camera glass

Sing, sirens—
sing *sweat* for us

and I too sing
for my food, your eyes
upon my arms, thighs, whatever
you ask of me, look at me

ii.

but Ragnarök is in my feed again
so I don't feel like actor or voyeur
this morning. I do not feel at all
made-up like the lush scream
of Death Valley superbloom in spring

and is there any mood more concussive
than melancholy in lingerie? God, let me be
Courtney, Lana, Apple but both body
& blush like scarred nectarine

unless, of course, I'm singing along
to Paula Cole, watching dust mites float
through late-day sunshine bent
by window pane, in which case, feed me
                              a sugar cube, cowboy

YOU CANNOT SAVE HERE

The *thunk* of a car door
behind me in the not-yet-
stretched pre-dawn half-light

still spring, still the chill
of up before the sun silence
on the edges of a base in Texas

still young, still a hungry, violent
sapling and startled by a snap-
second flash overhead, and a black

bird's body dropped at my boots
gone fast and almost vanishing
into asphalt under foot

My first omen just lies
there, a lecture on endings and how
they arrive, sudden and small

YOU CANNOT SAVE HERE

The sweat between
his belly and my back
sings two songs:
the divinity of being
pinned (*obvs*) and a hymn
hummed of the sunrise
still showing up after
cities start to topple

Why else bother
with latex, that second
skin, a lesson of the last
oblivion, the plague
which gave us
this tactile heritage
not something so careless
as hope, but, maybe, durability

STATEMENT OF TEACHING PHILOSOPHY

Sometimes I too
worry everything has been said
by those who got to the party early

I know
everyone has already fallen
in love despite a payload-painted sky

and I know
the world has been ending for
like, this whole time

but you
have people who want to smash
delivered to your pocket

and I
am worried you'll find me on Grindr
even if it's obvious I bottom

and did you realize
every love song ever written
can be folded up and carried

and even
the Bible borrowed language
already bobbing in the sublunar

listen
Nick Cave sews Orson Welles to Dickinson
and the Nobel went to a songwriter

so
just get out there and eat the day
we cyborgs—we superorganism

——

we've been brand
-new

LOVERS IN STONY RUN

Half-hidden in city shade
broken-tooth teenagers
certain they're fully ripe
flirt in an infected waterway
In too tight denim cutoffs, lovers
peacock their baby fat breasts
and washboard inexperience

She flings at her beloved
what she doesn't know is waste
water from upstream spillway
He sucks in runoff and sprays
a spit fountain, and summer
being summer, the brink of want
won't wait for unsoiled circumstance

You're glimmering he tells her
slicking swill from her shock of blonde
Their bodies leave little room for dog day
sweat, between them only wet
cotton tank, and the water hides
desire pressed to shorts steeped
in pollution too pretty to taste

They don't see us here he'll lie
and the city will turn
to hide its face

FRUIT OF THE UNENCLOSED LAND

"Remember the acorn;
It does not devour other acorns."
—Edgar Lee Masters

A friend leaving through the front door notices for the first time the poetry I wrote on a mirror at some point after I became the sort of person who writes poetry on their mirror. He asks about the Masters' quote, what it means to me, and I do my best to navigate the narrow social stream flowing between the woodlines of sentimentality and sincerity. He pauses, swishing my answer around in his mouth, considering the qualities of an acorn and nodding in the polite way that somehow forecasts *nah*.

The whole world eats, he tells me, *even the trees are squeezing each other out of space. It's a selfish world, of course, you know.* And so, again, I'm braced between two undressed landscapes—how rock doves can spot the selfish root of city gridlock, and how a fallen tree becomes a community that gives everything back. And along with the reluctant modernist, the words *crown shyness* and *mycorrhizal symbioses* bring out the bloom in me, even if I'm trying to origami each into some sort of guidon.

I don't know much about the acorn, but if I am to be a body, I wanna be a whole oak enveloped in kind potential. I no longer want to be the sort who shotguns the wolf because she shows her teeth.

TO THE PARENTS OF HITACHI SNAKE ROBOT

Pokémon Go is banned from
Fukushima nuclear disaster site

and even automata are drowning
in uranium floodwaters

The *suicide corps* is so small so someone's
built this 1:1 mock-up of the apocalypse

in a hangar up the road, and I wish
I could rehearse new geneses too

develop semiautomated solutions
for the problem of our fissile progress

A single dose of sievert is enough
to cause radiation sickness in humans

at seventy *Sv*, robots make deathbed conversions
so this reactor diver deserves a medal

A statesman writes a letter to the parents
of fallen drones *It is with great sorrow that…*

WHO MAKES IT

An ode to those Top Ramen
kids, latchkeys who knew
how to sex up a saucepan
lemon pepper, cayenne
when to drain and how

one for the squeegee boys
and Kool-Aid stands, both
trying to hustle the summer
on sidewalks & through
streets and code reds

one for the mallrats
with empty wallets
wasting warm days
getting shoplifting looks
inside a Sharper Image

an ode to everyone
who bought non-slick
black sneaks in their teens
and scuffed them up
on film-thick linoleum

Over our 15-and-a-comp-meal
we form a world-wide choir
of unwelcome animals—just as you
are a lost one, I am an opossum
we beasts shall inherit the ruins

THE LEXICON OF SOMMELIERS

I apologize for worshiping
the way the words *cotillion*
bouquet feel like a whole cherry
tomato held in a closed mouth

I'm sorry the trailer park has become
metonym for poverty and poverty
for labor but utility longs
for uselessness like

a lexicon of sommeliers:
mouthfeel, must, disgorge, plonk and port
nothing I need but a song I want
to steal, uncork, pound down and pair

with a bottle's throat stuffed
with kerosene tea towel hooked
into rococo oriel—this unrest
must be sonant

give us a birdsong
give us a goddamn
give us a brand new
glossolalia

THESE 10 WEIRD TRICKS WILL CHANGE YOUR WORKPLACE FOREVER

Do one thing each day
that scares the bosses

Mention the march
Mention motherhood

Learn to love your ugly
lack of utility

Remember Curiosity sings to herself
humming *happy birthday* in red planet exile

Be rose hip staining the teeth
of unsympathetic gear trains

Fill a disposable project
full of waged minutes

Write poetry at your desk
addressed to office Xerox

Close up shop for an hour
to stare at the sun

Be honest with colleagues
about the terror blotting you out

ASKING FOR PrEP

The nurse asks me about risk factors, and
I don't tell her that sometimes love is shaped
like fingers folded into fists that feel
like the brink between pinch and seized piston

Instead I say I was

born during the plague
under the sign of the pig
which makes me young enough
for panic to have never kissed me like that

but old enough to worry constantly
every time my body is gifted and split
and I call it safer but I cannot pretend
I don't know men unwound down to bone

I know it's better now, but I describe why
I can barely afford sex that doesn't kill me
how we are tender and raw, tendon and maw
and the terror of asking feels half new to me

I'm sorry—I tell her—I'm not usually this optimistic

POLY BEACH HOUSE

a thin film floats over the weekend

an unerotic tension of sucked stomachs
and bathroom breaks snuck in while
the rest stroll on the boardwalk

and one of us allows her ache for tasting
everything to overwhelm the ever-present
whisper of the end of the season

and one of us says nothing as she slips
out to watch the sun rise
over an ocean that loathes us

and one of us says they're scared
the undine inside won't be seen
before the moon collides with the sea

and all of us feel it. After a swim
I carve ἔσχατος in the sand, and my body
wishes I had the time to cover up my bad

tattoos—O apocalypse, we just want
a summer. When wasn't The End
hiding behind the sun?

A JUMPMASTER IN DUPONT CIRCLE

and their spears into pruning hooks
—Isaiah 2:4

I baulk to baptize him with any sound
that feels too familiar on a queer tongue

a *bear* is not a fit, nor a *daddy*
hairy and holding both grit and glitter

at the downtown orgy of sound and rouge
painted nails recalled fingered trigger

he used to teach the body to fall
he said as he squeezed his boots into heels

used to stand on the edge of firmament
inspecting the sky for snags, and shout

now he greets with kisses on cheeks
all who wander their way to the circle

Jumpers, hit it. Get it, girls. This daylight
will transmute our weapons back into boys

AFTER STAR STUFF

Praise be Saint Sagan
for the explosion that killed figurative language

Because, I am the furnace
and yes, I am a bustier

Still, you are the cellar
Yes, you are the end of days

LUDDITE

"I would bring a hammer."
—Jan Hein Donner, Chess Grandmaster

Internet oracles declare the end
of work—LIGHTS OUT
for a bright tomorrow!

No more toiling over
the lever dilemma—our scientists
solved philosophy for automated cars!

And the self-checkout punches the clock
having fought a boss for the hour
she needs to get to her second job

And the synchronized production line
protests the lack of heat, air
and daytime television in the factory

So we've cracked labor just in time
and thinking, generally, and time
to let go of recreation soon

Next let's make us a mechanical
Ned Ludd, an automaton with two
able arms waving our black flags for us

DROWNING IS AN APPARENT AND UNEXPECTED RECURRENT CAUSE OF MASS MORTALITY OF COMMON STARLINGS

Too many poems begin
with murmurations and awe

not nearly enough with baths
of glossy, waterlogged wings

the human kingdoms decree
a crisis of despair

we respond with a hashtag:
#IfIWereTheHappinessMinister

the starling doesn't share
our love for crowned heads

as far as we can tell
as far as we can tell

it's worship: of bodies
of water

YOU CANNOT SAVE HERE

To be conscious is to be
a monster, an absolute unit

of measurement for distrust
as in // language is a gatdam

guillotine, no try again // language
is a missing kitchen knife

as in // put a shiv of specificity
in abstraction's blistered hands

as in you're sitting in one of those
unrenovated Dunkins looking

into strip mall asphalt, gray day
in mid-June, too young

to do much about harbor
water algae bloom and besides

you don't own a car
and the future's too far to walk

as in // every lb. a thousand
on those long lags between trees

on summer streets, concrete eats
optimism and the backs of your knees

sweat like there's no tomorrow
one more try // language is lagniappe

you're sure there's a word for this disquiet
but—listen—

A BODY IN PRETTY BOY

Summer ends like an eighties film
what's left of a body recovered from the top

of a reservoir. The news reports little
except to repeat an edict: *no swimming*

and at Loch Raven, a whole town has been given up
to the waters—every reservoir has a horror story

Here hidden a drowned village, quarry, steeple, silo
within: sunken Warren, Milford, Vantage, Monte Ne

police boats skim a surface reflecting pious cottonwood
at the banks, on their knees, before an inverted sky

below, a homestead gathers
to welcome the sun's slow departure

WRATH OF A QUEER GOD

The first ones to go would be the tasteless, anyone who has wielded un-rhymed sacred text as armament, made body holey with Leviticus or even denied a name at holiday dinner. I'd be an Old Testament type—no, Greek—know fear as I cast down my wisdom in the form of light-ning bolts, flooding Southern towns that build billboards for blond Jesus. Thou shall have no other before me in hairy legs and platform heels. Next I'd come for the trailer parks (not that the salt of the earth have wronged, but to deny the shame of my own genesis) leaving only the baby butch toughs to testify, to reinscribe the words *awesome* and *enormity* with the weight they're due. The rich, I'd eat whole, consuming capital and shitting out bread and boutique health clinics. This hunger not only devastates, but lets rise thrift store monarchs, the most clever among you, now kings in their knock-off luxury, now queens in their shoplifted MAC. I'd tear to timber every suburban church, in part for their precepts but more for their aesthetic—how dare build anything but peacocked glory, stone and glass phalluses. Look now to the lesbian witches in hiking boots—let them show you what structures the moon desires.

I am everything you say you say I am. Witness my agenda: shade and spite, swallowing men whole.

YOU CANNOT SAVE HERE

The flock scratch an unsteady
streak across speckled evening orange

this season, skies sneak off
knowing futures are down all over

a skein as a train horn haunting
with the promise of somewhere safer

our feet tethered to asphalt and obligation
we fault their flight as cowardice

cerulean warblers, black rail, no name
more gorgeous than *elsewhere*

II.

Sunset? He might at least wait and see if there's a tomorrow morning.

—Dhalgren, Samuel R. Delany (1975)

YOU CANNOT SAVE HERE

Let me start again—
I mean I want
to flee with you

I want you to shoot me
in that end-times lighting
instead of me stealing one

last selfie in a home
-made face mask against long
burnt-out neon billboard barely

still showing *Domino Sugars*
When the mob bum-rushes
the flour and paper towels

we bolt; I'll start by keeping watch
out the back window when we rumble
away from old world, post-home city

I mean *wherever elsewhere*
as long as we can touch

YOU CANNOT SAVE HERE

Morning gets angry and destroys a city
not New York, too obvious, but suppose
it's on the coast. Suppose we're the first to go

I picture Goya's Colossus and my empathy
runs threadbare. Suppose I notice the raw meat
of his back and fall in love. Suppose

there are too few Armageddon songs
about giants. The Norse, I suppose,
and Nephilim, okay, fine, so suppose

what I want are more movies: *Colossus*
starring Dwayne "The Rock" Johnson
we'd see it in dim theatres, giant screen

and afterward, step into the parking garage's
echo and oilslick, a perspective behind concrete
and absence of concrete, brutalists framing

for the aftermath of Morning, or giant
or indifference—our skyline swapped
with fields of dandelion left unattended

YOU CANNOT SAVE HERE

After Lars von Trier

My favorite apocalypse
starts with an orphan planet
starts with a wedding
starts with a star somewhere
south of where it should be

My favorite apocalypse
knows sadness refuses
to work for circumstance
but who wouldn't want
washed in lavish sorrow

to spend The End
tucked in taffeta
gown as the sky bows
to kiss an emerald lawn
like vow-bound believer

When we collide I want
sent off as my worst self
wrapped in black basque riding
cross-eyed cub caught in sand trap
unvexed by endtimes hailstorm

My favorite apocalypse
consolidates water bottle, takeout
straw, SIM card, Chemex, combustion
engine, fast-fashion black jacket,
apple orchard, first born

not a breath left to ask
Are you happy? Aren't you happy?

YOU CANNOT SAVE HERE

Would brooding over a Doré woodcut offer any insight on what jetsam comes washing into your cul-de-sac when 19,000 miles of shoreline go under? When the sea comes knocking on city doors | as your sixteen-miles-to-the-gallon four-by-four slowly folds the distance between my home and yours | I'm out

> stoop-perched elder
> fans away
> fevered September

catch me cutting a modern life from your half-acre dream of isolation | I'm there, misassembling my Swedish couch between your pickup and SUV | If you're frightened by the half-shaved bears hosting our nude bacchanal on your front lawn | just wait for the OWLs perched on your porch, delivering lectures on Rich and hooks to your daughters

> uncollared cat
> basking atop abandoned sedan:
> fireflies appear

it's true I too drink from permanent debris, combust too quickly and often | I am not doomed any differently than you | but denial makes fault a throwable stone | so we're loading up the cities two-by-two | call me Charon, steering our ark toward the suburbs and every monster has a ticket—A throng of fey boys with glittered bat wings—the boogeymen made of the word "urban"—every ghost of American indifference

> murine shadows
> abdicate
> as warm rain arrives

YOU CANNOT SAVE HERE

After "Men standing with pile of buffalo skulls,
Michigan Carbon Works"

    a.

That photo from the textbooks—
  you remember, their skulls heaped
  by the thousands, a horned mound
  itself a monster when squinting

  and a suit standing on top
  claiming dominion, a sepia
  memento that there's nothing
  the beast West won't extinguish

—it tells us that this isn't the first
last days. Here near the end
of the sixth extinction, finality
gets sold in bulk

    b.

The moonscape of West Virginia
is now, hiding just behind hemlock
pine beauty lines, and the chop
of rotorcraft sings the indigenous names

  of here's holocaust. Or a camp in the plains
  a middle passage. an atom splitting
  two cities, like—maybe here's
  been wrong too long; today's

a monument worth toppling
Like Oppenheimer, apple-myth
Newton was into the metaphysic
you know? Had World to Come
math worked out in shorthand

and 2060 is around the corner
now and seems a bit generous
at this point—this song's proportions
have bloated. Let us start again

    c.

on bent card with blemished edge
the skeletal rider on a pale horse
will usually herald a gasp, but
it reminds us not every ending

invites calamity, and since we're talking
Rider-Waite-Smith, we're talking
a trampled king, and if we're talking
about the sublimity of climax, I can't

not mention the palette of orange
in John Martin's apocalypse, even if
I'm not a theist. I know not
every ending brings brimstone

—c'mon, no, not like paradise
not like Zion, like *there has to be something
better than man. Has to be.* Like five
sci-fi films forming a causal loop, like

> *Now the artist who painted that picture
> said that something was missing, what is it?
> 'It is I myself, who was part of the landscape
> I painted'*

YOU CANNOT SAVE HERE

My favorite apocalypse
is a photo, a single shot of the end
of the boardwalk, swallowed
by the storm's autumn holiday

What she leaves is just spectacle
skeleton of tubular steel and some time
after the storm, a believer scales the Star
Jet's frame to post the Stars & Stripes

our ugliest impulse, to colonize
even The End, collapse, making claim
on apocalyptic monuments, as if
nations still stand a chance

Give us The End's composition
as it lies—the sunrise tucked
between the coils of metallic sea
serpent, uninterpreted

YOU CANNOT SAVE HERE

After Rukeyser and Mann

Don't look up
from the text when the water laps
at the sill like polite Poseidean missionary

Remember the only gospel our parents' lost
decades gave us was learning to love
the despised backsides of houses

and what mark will the city herself leave
when she retreats? A variegated bloom?
A morning-after bruise?

What I'm asking is:
how long can I sit here, *Save Me*
playing as the carpets drink up The End?

The door is unlocked—
come read Rukeyser with me
until the lights flicker out

YOU CANNOT SAVE HERE

After Skeeter Davis

My favorite apocalypse
is a song about breaking up

bc sure, the shore is arriving
soon, and we haven't even started

tidying up yet, and yes, men
are gathering with American

flag vinyl wraps on their rifles
yes, a plague, yes, a mob

yes, yet there are still young lovers
leaving, leaving forty-one missed calls

on a Friday night, and nineteen
voicemails quilting together

heartstring vocals breaking
through a cell phone receiver

Who hasn't been either
end at some point, the listener

the left behind, the song itself
so I'm sorry if sometimes, I sing

along to doomsday kitsch when
she says *it ended when you said goodbye*

Our shithead hearts won't stop
for something so small as collapse

YOU CANNOT SAVE HERE

The few others who washed up
here with us passed away from
boredom and despair
—Cid Del Norte Marquez

My favorite apocalypse
happens halfway through
as in, everything comes down
and you've got to keep going

as in, you are witness
to the trappings of classic
catastrophe: a shake, a shock-
wave, separation, your memories

split open and what's left
is a pitch you recognize
as the wind and an undone coast
that whispers behind you: *loss. loss*

a whole year has passed
everything washed in an autumn
palette and a dove or dying elder
insists an elsewhere and someone

you knew is alive out there
and you've got to keep going

YOU CANNOT SAVE HERE

The seams burst, and we still have to go to work. The waters rise and someone still asks you to put on a boot or tie, a smile, black slacks and/or sneaks, sell your hours while the West turns to ash, while the world covers a hacking cough.

Gozer takes a downtown tower & cops refuse to shut down traffic along Pratt Street during rush hour. A rider appears on a dark horse on the beltway's west-bound lane & a thousand locusts swarm around each hoof as it hits the asphalt. The skies turn grey—the radio hums an annual fundraising drive.

Your boss sucks his teeth on the other end of a call: *unprecedented times*, yes yes, *new normal* yes yes, *I hope this finds you well*—Fenrir stretches upward on his hind legs to swallow the sun—*just take care*
                    to find someone
                              who can cover your shift

III.

The principle of hope operates wherever people foresee a cataclysm that will put an end to the established order so that a new, purified reality can appear.

The Witness of Poetry,
Czeslaw Milosz (1983)

YOU CANNOT SAVE HERE

I found myself well-dressed and drunk on free
shiraz, the night of the most recent war:
a friend came through with seats for two to see
an opera now set here in Baltimore
the same day I witnessed sewn fruit displayed
as art—the sculptor said that assembly
gave her the space to grow, that it relayed
her ache for friends unglued by HIV
I asked the museum if end-of-days
plans were in place in case of disaster,
"whose job is it to grab the two Monets
should docents abandon the old masters
when, I don't know, cluster bomb start to drop?"
a calm hand stroked my back, whispered, "Love—stop"

YOU CANNOT SAVE HERE

The day was grave enough that we stopped talking about all other apocalypses, somewhere there around the Worm Moon and the end of Mercury's spin in the wrong direction. The car speaker had a hard time getting in a word about a new KIA in a war they said had ended, but considered how the outbreak may be cousin to the other catastrophes down the road. You looked at me over center console, flipped off the radio, and asked me to read you a poem. I read a BA recipe instead and said a pandemic was a bad time to hookup in a Penn Pike rest stop. We sent texts to the new lovers we were seeing back home, then spoke sweetly of kissing their hands after everyone had washed them. I mumbled a meditation on polyamory in an Armageddon, for new fingers inside us in the time of social distancing, scrubbed for 20 seconds before rinsing, just the time it takes to whisper the chorus to *stayin' alive. Stayin' alive.*

YOU CANNOT SAVE HERE

After Zeitlin, Alibar and Stevens

*"For the animals that didn't have a dad to put them in the boat,
the end of the world already happened."*
—Hushpuppy, Beasts of the Southern Wild

i.   the truth is a group of crows
     is called whatever you want, poet
     call it a flock, name it a summer
     an apocalypse, a sacred text

     I ask my students to turn down
     the volume then I go home
     get high, write about doomsday
     fires blinking on the horizon

ii. consider the hummingbird
     corpse I saw on campus today
     just outside the tall windows
     that welcome light into our classrooms

     its faded plumage no longer
     a shimmer in the air but avocado
     green and black, barely a smear
     on flecked asphalt

iii. The End is gorgeous
     like everything that can kill us:
     scorpion, palisade, may bells, oil
     rainbowing the surface of the sea

iv.   the horse chestnut
down past the post office
fills with a hundred corvids
so I take the long way around

Having left my glasses at home
I look up, mistake starlings
in the brass light for the bats
who roost beneath the interstate

v.   our resolve takes the form of tattoos
hog or cock or FEMA x-code
a mark to remind us of a shore
somewhere, still out of sight

vi.   the truth is The End happens
all the time, every day
a diagnosis, an eviction
a bullet, a bullet, a bullet

vii.   and something intimate waits for us
in the bottom of the crock pot soup
you started before the emergency
alert squealed from your phone

viii.   I introduce you
to a board game about the end
of days, and you laugh, ask
if it's called *Monopoly*

ix.   I use vacant as a noun
my city fills with red brick
row home plywood windows
bandaging abandoned pasts

x.   the truth is our dog
is going to slow us down
and may be a barrier for entry
at northern border crossings

her chipped smile justifies
the risk, and we ask ourselves
what weight is worth drowning
trying to carry home

xi.   every bird becomes a vulture
every animal a scavenger
every tooth in our clutch
of pearls shaped to tear

xii.   the truth is The End
isn't here yet
the truth is The End
has already begun

xiii.   vigilant on the concrete lip
the blackbird remains unphased
by the panic of footsteps
slapping across a parking lot

YOU CANNOT SAVE HERE

After The Truman Show

I rewatch *The Truman Show*
during quarantine

and that actress who is playing
an actress is wearing a button

that says "How's it Going to End?"
and two things happen; first

I burst like a goddamn
egg, I unknot like an egg, I weep

like an egg. I succeed at being
a mess, and two, I realize that after Truman

takes a bow and steps
into the black, that world

they've built there, must end
Too many shows go on

for too long—the Fonz
jumps over a shark

someone wins the lottery
but it was all a dream

Bless the curtain:
Some ends of some worlds

are meant to be, I think
a happy ending

HOW TO WRITE A LOVE POEM
DURING A PLAGUE

First, don't

but remember
that this too shall
be settled, accepted
one day as standard:
an intimacy absent
of the sweat and ugly
scents that make it
Discover you miss
stripping off a pit-
soaked t-shirt between
unceasing lips

Next, try not to

fall for someone new
and if you do, I guess
the talk about safer-
sex sounds different
(unless you survived
the '80s). You know
what, just wash
your hands or learn
to long or fuck long-
distance. I don't
know what day it is
but the moon is
still waxing
even if you and I
have stopped shaving

Finally, go ahead

and say it: I've worn this
hoodie for four days, and I
miss you, I
think

YOU CANNOT SAVE HERE

There's so much more you
and I, now that *outside*
and *elsewhere* are missing

We keep the windows
open during daylight
to ensure we're still here

and our tree continues
to yoke itself with pink
until it falls for the sidewalk

Accordingly, at night we flip
a coin to decide who wears
a tux and who lipstick

The blossoms continue
their peep show
with or without witness

YOU CANNOT SAVE HERE

After Rilke and Fauci

After 148 days inside
stacked, end-to-end
from hoodie and heater
to straining central air
I reconsider the body

problem. On one hand
who needs hands, a ribcage
stuffed with disquiet
the soft tissue of desire
that dark center where

the narrative gets jammed up
but, fuck, do you remember
the four of us, and both dogs
tucked into a hatchback, howling
Dolly lyrics 'til we went raspy?

Or do you recall stone
soup picnics in the park?
The mosquitos mauling my leg
as we passed my favorite gay
poems back and forth in the grass

You held open the thin book with one
hand, pulled a pit from your sucking lips
with the other. I used my index
fingernail to press tiny crosses
into the raised pink of my skin

YOU CANNOT SAVE HERE

There were no new tattoos, no more *memento mori*
that haunted summer—we sat on a stoop

I wiped my damp hands
on the pages of clenched-fist memoirs,
and you swore you saw a maimed sweetgum
carve *FAAFO* into its trunk. I said

let's be ugly, you and I
and I wanna smell like living
and you, and you wanna smell like the sun
marinating wave after wave of black and red banners

I wanna share disorderly stone fruit
& lob what's left on a cop car

YOU CANNOT SAVE HERE

And it came to pass in those days
a certain soccer team made us forget
how wicked our flags were while

outside, on my block, two wise women
hunched on the stoop became
one lonely woman on a stoop

What I'm saying is The End
takes his time. Summer slogs
on with Mid-Atlantic malice

while somewhere deep in the city
park, ungentle waterfowl swallow
Frito-Lay lilypads and sing nothing

I crave in the shade and hope
for a less cruel collapse
swipe right and wait for sundown

I cannot tell you what to name me
after dark in a pile of final months
I only know that I don't identify

as the moon or the night
but as silhouette of blackbird against
slate dark sky over rowhome cornice

What I'm saying is I was just
out walking, and I'm scared
and, love, lock the door. Lock the door

AFTER *THE LAST GENERATION*

"I think when the Marshall Islands will be gone, it's like the end of life to me—the end of the world."
—Wilmer Joel, age 12, future president of the Marshall Islands

It is no comfort to know
the sky is darker elsewhere
and the sandwich board

soothsayer trope of '90s cinema
is technically already right
given the frequency of pale skin

's arrival as forecast for ruin
Which is to say: The End
need not look like Dürer

's riders, ours instead a simple
stupid cruelty: mismanagement
of oceans, peoples, futures, anger

a legacy of fist-shaped holes
in the walls of other people
's homes, nations, futures

It is no comfort to know the coasts
hum, resentful—one sea sings
of being fed shackled bodies

the other says nothing, a half-
life memory, a dozen atolls
gnashed by atom and evacuated

It is no comfort to know
I come from a long line
of pale horses

YOU CANNOT SAVE HERE

In the end
the good news is the end
is not The End—not in the sense
of the gospel, but the spirit
of second growth

Over the edge
bees are blessed with another chance
pirouetting over our fossiled progress
honeycombing remains of skeletal steel
triumphant on grass-fractured boulevards

BOTTICELLI PAINTS HIS FEARS

Our feeds hummed
a moratorium on rimming

and we saw nothing new
that wasn't online—everyone

there was quoting Yeats
anyway, so we went for a walk

I asked if you knew the origin
of the word *millennial*

you said nothing & pointed toward
two crust punks picnicking

on the stones near where
the river sinks beneath the city

Behind them, the storm
drain was decorated

with Botticelli's angels
and I swear the yogurt sky

insisted to the evening
we were living in—if not

the end of days—at least
an end of days

YOU CANNOT SAVE HERE

After Eileen Myles

What are you supposed to be
tweeting during the storm?

The thing about history
is we forget how

often we are sitting in the living
room when it happens

You are mashing the buttons
on the remote you

still haven't replaced
the batteries in

when it happens. I know
your phone makes you feel

like you're there, but you're not
there. You just turned the stove off

and there's winter light coming
through the blinds, but it's

quiet where you are, when
it happens. You are wishing

      (*did you turn the stove off?*)

you bought better bread
when it happens. Your

      (*go make sure you turned the stove off*)

dog needs a walk and
your grilled cheese

is getting anxious
when it happens

There's this elder who says
it's hard to figure out

what's poetry and what's
a tweet at this time, and

it's true that you're not really
sure what happens next either

YOU CANNOT SAVE HERE

The seven hundredth day of The End
I don't do anything—let my circadian

rhythm slip loose by rising
with the midday hum of lunch

rush bustle outside city window
Sweater weather in December suggests

The End continues to sputter along
slowly enough we don't panic at its approach

I roll myself out of plush nest and pour
an afternoon coffee as winter spills

the golden hour early, and I spring
myself into evening, then night

then the hours when even the moon
puts her phone away, when I'm feeling

like the only person left on a broken
planet—sometimes, I keep the lights out

stand in the center of carpeted blue rooms
during the witching hour, wonder

what I'm doing with myself, and it's not
that we were wrong about it all coming

down, it's that we've gotten used to it
No sudden flood, no final kiss

just the slow goodbye of ice
in a sweating rocks glass

here, then less here
then not here

YOU CANNOT SAVE HERE

After Jane Hirshfield

Looking back, let them catalog
a people with hands

Let them catalog
the waves, the shoreline
Louisiana losing its boot

Let them catalog
moments too small
to stack, steel water
bottles, bulk bins
of flax seed

Let them catalog, assuming
there will be a future *them*
a *we* that didn't freeze inside
a quickening cone of light

Let them catalog
something more than a finger
wagged at overweight pickup
trucks and fits of silence
at holiday dinners

Let them catalog
manure lagoons returning
their slurry to uncontrolled
flood waters

Let them catalog
you and I, still reading
paperbacks in our rowhome
a video fireplace crackling
on a flatscreen

Let them catalog
mothers writing poems
to tell their children
of their inaction

Let them catalog Paradise
California as ashes smeared
across a map

Let them catalog
Doggerland, Dresden, Centralia
Baghdad, Tangier Island
Hispaniola, home

Let them catalog
a forest of windmills
stretching across the Mojave

Let them catalog
one end of days interrupting
another, a tornado warning
during a quarantine

Let them catalog forestallment
or ask *how could you?*

Let them catalog
a past that did not blink

AUBADE FOR AN ENDING
THAT DOESN'T ARRIVE

There are mornings (the rare mornings
when you're up before the heat, on walks
or rides out to an urban reservoir
belted by wildflower and spike iron
fence, belted by bike path, belted by
thoroughfare, belted by row-home
tucked into city misremembered
by everyone except the six a.m. sun
summoning the hum of human
and roadway churn, slowly at first
so as not to shock the stillness still
lingering, nautical dawn left settled
on bus stop bench, on unwashed
marble stoop step, on those
trees near the low-rise housing
on Caroline Street where someone
some management someone, some
unromantic government has trimmed
them to nothing but tall trunks, freed
of any ornament, leaf, stem, branch
like the reservoir, where, while
blessing the water for future use
workers stirred it until unpotable
and the bike path is halved
which makes the odd marble
tower feel out of the city's way
an accidental setting, not a place
you aim, but somewhere you
stumble, but an old jogger
has stopped there, in firstlight
with half the city sprawling
out below, and hands-on-hips
he tells you how community once

fought to keep it up, just so
the two of you, standing here
as the city wakes up, could
pause) when you imagine
a world that ends more
slowly, a world where
The End never arrives at all

THE CITY THAT RETURNS IS THE CITY

i.   I walk by a body, sprawled out
in the grass, in a park that's been
empty for a year, and there's
something about spring that summons
savasana before *corpse*

There's a hubris in the crocuses
littering color across the city
in the tail end of the plague year, in
the tail end of the Anthropocene
The city that returns is the city

that was before. For better or worse
The world that returns is still dying

ii.   I'm not out here trying to be
a poet who writes about flowers
Just—Hermes loved a boy so much he tags
his man's name in thawing parks every April:
purple crown, golden halo, perennial bottom

iii.   The crocus' hubris
rhymes with optimism
The spring sings the same myth as the fall:
you cannot save here

NOTES

"Enjoy yourself—it's later than you think" is a line from a song of the
   same name by Carl Sigman and Herb Magidson.

"Wenn du mich siehst, dann weine" translates to "if you see me,
   weep." It is taken from a carving found in a centuries-old "hunger
   stone" found on the banks of the Elbe River. The carving com-
   memorates historic droughts throughout the years. When the
   water in the river is high, the stone remains hidden. When the
   water is low enough, as it is during droughts, the inscription is re-
   vealed, warning of hardship in the days to come.

"So Eden sank to Grief / So dawn goes down to day" is a line taken
   from Robert Frost's poem "Nothing Gold Can Stay."

Ways of Seeing is a 1972 television series by John Berger.

"One wild and precious life" is a fragment taken from Mary Oliver's
   poem "The Summer Day."

"Remember the acorn; / It does not devour other acorns" is a line
   taken from Edgar Lee Masters' poem "Robert Davidson."

Pokémon Go is a mobile-based video game that really is banned from
   the Fukushima nuclear disaster site. Hitachi Snake Robot is a
   robot developed by Hitachi to support clean up of that site. Sv is
   the abbreviation for sievert, which is a unit of ionizing radiation
   dose. The "suicide corps" is one name given to the group of volun-
   teers, mostly elders, who offered their services at the radiated site
   after the 2011 incident.

Curiosity is the name of one of NASA's rover designed to study the
   Gale crater on Mars.

PrEP is an acronym and the common term for pre-exposure prophy-
   laxis, a daily medication that can significantly reduce the chances
   of getting HIV.

"and their spears into pruning hooks" is a line taken from the Bible.

"Saint Sagan" refers to astronomer Carl Sagan, the person most re-
   sponsible for the idea that "we are made of star stuff."

"I would bring a hammer" is the answer that chess grandmaster Jan
   Hein Donner gave when asked how he would prepare to play
   against a supercomputer.

"Drowning is an Apparent and Unexpected Recurrent Cause of Mass Mortality of Common Starlings" takes its title from a scientific article of the same name.

"After Lars von Trier" responds to the film *Melancholia*.

"Goya's Colossus" refers to Francisco de Goya's early 1800 painting "The Colossus."

"Men standing with pile of buffalo skulls, Michigan Carbon Works" refers to a historic photo held in the Burton Historic Collection of the Detroit Public Library. In that same poem "Oppenheimer" refers to J. Robert Oppenheimer, who helped America create its first atomic weapons. "Newton" refers to physicist Sir Isaac Newton, who held deeply religious views about the end of days. In 1704, Newton predicted that the world would end in 2060. "Rider-Waite-Smith" refers to one of the most popular tarot decks. "John Martin's apocalypse" refers to a series of end-times paintings from the English painter. The two quotes that end the poem are taken from the science fiction films *Planet of the Apes* (1968) and *Escape from the Planet of the Apes* (1971).

"My favorite apocalypse / is a photo…" refers to several photos taken of the Jet Star Roller Coaster in Seaside Heights, New Jersey after Hurricane Sandy.

"After *The Truman Show*" refers to the 1998 film *The Truman Show*.

Beasts of the Southern Wild is a 2012 film based on the play *Juicy and Delicious*. The poem inspired by this film also takes formal inspiration from the poem "Thirteen Ways of Looking at a Blackbird" by Wallace Stevens.

Cid Del Norte Marquez is a fictional character from the video game Final Fantasy VI (originally released as Final Fantasy 3 in the U.S.).

Gozer is a fictional character from the 1984 film *Ghostbusters*. Fenrir is a figure of Norse mythology who plays an important part in that eschatology.

The artist whose work is referred to in the poem that begins "I found myself well dressed…" is Zoe Leonard.

"A Doré woodcut" refers to Gustave Doré's woodcuts. In that same poem, OWL is an older LGBTQ+ acronym that stands for "older, wiser lesbian." Related, "Rich and hooks" refers to feminist writers Adrienne Rich and bell hooks. Charon is the boatman who carries souls across the river that divides the world of the living from the world of the dead.

The Last Generation is an award-winning interactive documentary by Michelle Mizner and Katie Worth. It documents the stories of three children living

on the Marshall Islands. In that same poem, "Dürer's riders" refers
to Albrecht Dürer's famous woodcut *The Four Horsemen, From the
Apocalypse.*

In "Poly Beach House," ἔσχατος is ancient Greek and translates to
"end times."

"The despised backsides of houses" is a fragment taken from the poem
"Despisals" by Muriel Rukeyser. "Save Me" refers to the 1999 song
from Aimee Mann.

"The dark center where" is a fragment taken from the poem "Archaic
Torso of Apollo" by Rainer Maria Rilke.

FAAFO stands for "fuck around and find out."

"Botticelli Paints His Fears" is a phrase taken from a magazine article
titled "Ten Notable Apocalypses That (Obviously) Didn't Hap-
pen." The article discusses the painting "The Mystical Nativity," by
Sandro Botticelli, at the top of which the painter includes an end-
times warning. In that same poem, Yeats refers to the Irish poet
W.B. Yeats, particularly his famous apocalyptic poem "The Second
Coming."

"Stayin' Alive" is a 1977 hit single from the Bee Gees. During the out-
break of COVID-19, several sources recommended washing one's
hands for the length it takes to hum the chorus of this song. The
song has also been used as a way to measure the pace at which
chest compressions should be administered during CPR.

"It ended when you said, goodbye" is a line from the Skeeter Davis'
1962 song "The End of the World."

"It's hard to figure out what's poetry and what's a tweet at this time" is
a quote from Eileen Myles in their 2015 interview for The Art of
Poetry series from *The Paris Review.*

"After Jane Hirschfield" refers to Hirshfield's poem "Let Them Not
Say" and follows a similar structure.

One myth of the origin of the crocus flower is that there was a mortal
named Crocus who was lover and companion to Hermes, herald of
the gods. While engaged in athletic pursuits, Hermes accidentally
beheaded Crocus with a misthrown discus. In grief, Hermes
turned Crocus into the flower, which is one of the first to bloom as
winter gives way to spring.

Late in the process of writing & editing of these poems, I realized that there are two earlier works titled "My favorite apocalypse," a line that appears repeatedly in this book. One is a collection of poems by Catie Rosemurgy, and the other is a collection of speculative fiction. Though I wasn't aware of these works when I was writing, I should give these folks credit for arriving at the same phrase as I did (and before I did).

ACKNOWLEDGEMENTS

An earlier version of "A Jumpmaster in DuPont Circle" originally
   appeared in the Winter 2018 issue of *Little Patuxent Review*.
An earlier version of "After Star Stuff" originally appeared in the
   Spring 2016 issue of *Minetta Review*.
"You Cannot Save Here" (After Lars von Trier) appeared in the
   Summer 2019 issue of *Voicemail Poems*.
"You Cannot Save Here" ("Morning gets angry and destroys a city")
   appeared in *Hobart Literary Journal* in September 2019.
"You Cannot Save Here" ("My favorite apocalypse happens halfway
   through") appeared in *Cartridge Lit* in December 2019.
"Aubade for An Ending That Doesn't Arrive" appeared in the Mary-
   land's Writers Association's 2020 Anthology.
"Who Makes It" and "Drowning is an Apparent and Unexpected Re-
   current Cause of Mass Mortality of Common Starlings" appeared
   in the Spring 2020 issue of *Poet Lore*.
The poem "Wrath of a Queer God" appeared the anthology *Glitter +
   Ashes: Queer Tales of a World That Wouldn't Die*.
"A Body in Pretty Boy" appeared in issue 38 of *Windfall Room*.
*A selection of these poems was honored with the 2019 Adele V. Holden
   Prize for creative excellence.*

Thank you to all of these publications and organizations who have
shared and celebrated the poems that appear in this book.

Thank you to Washington Writers' Publishing House members both
past and present for making this book possible, especially those poets
who selected my work as the winner of the Jean Feldman Poetry Prize
and helped to polish the manuscript. Though it is a stacked lineup of
poets over there, I'd like to say specifically that it has been a pleasure to
once again work with Steven Leyva, a poet and editor whose work I
admire.

Thank you to my entire writing community. Literature is not plucked from the ether or delivered by spirits. It is built by people living in a community and engaging with other readers and writers, both in person and on the page. Thank you to everyone who offered feedback on any of these poems earlier in the process, particularly the members of my writing group, The Healthies. I'd also like to offer a shoutout to Meg Day, Dora Malech and Sarah Pinsker for taking the time to offer their kind praise for us to include on the back cover. Of course, I cannot speak of community without also thanking my poetry educators and mentors, both formal and informal, especially Kendra Kopelke, Ishion Hutchinson, and celeste doaks.

I'm so grateful to work with Andrew Sargus Klein on this book's cover. He is brilliant, and he is patient. Andrew and I are both grateful to Geography of Robots for allowing us to use their art for the cover.

Finally, thank you to my partner: my first reader and my best friend.

DR. TONEE MAE MOLL is a queer & trans writer & educator. Her debut memoir, *Out of Step*, won the 2018 Lambda Literary Award, and was featured that year on the American Library Association's annual list of notable LGBTQ+ books. Tonee Mae's poetry has also received the Adele V. Holden award for creative excellence and the Bill Knott Poetry Prize. She has been a finalist for the Baker Award, and her work has been nominated for the Pushcart Prize and Best of Net. She holds a PhD in English from Morgan State University and an MFA in creative writing & publishing art from University of Baltimore. Her scholarly work explores feminist pedagogies & epistemologies, poetry, and punk. She is, most notably, a Gemini.

Washington Writers' Publishing House is a non-profit, cooperative literary organization that has published over 100 volumes of poetry since 1975 as well as fiction and nonfiction. The press sponsors three annual competitions for writers living in DC, Maryland, and Virginia, and the winners of each category (poetry, fiction, and creative nonfiction) comprise our annual slate. In 2021, WWPH launched an online literary journal, *WWPH Writes*, to expand our mission to further the creative work of writers in our region. In 2024, WWPH launched its biennial Works in Translation series. More about the Washington Writers' Publishing House is at www.washingtonwriters.org.